With Love

To _____

From _____

secrets of
LOVE

J. Donald Walters

Hardbound edition, first printing 1993

Copyright 1993
J. Donald Walters

Illustration Copyright © 1993 Crystal Clarity, Publishers

ISBN 1-56589-035-3

PRINTED IN HONG KONG

Crystal Clarity
P U B L I S H E R S

14618 Tyler Foote Road, Nevada City, CA 95959
1 (800) 424-1055

A seed thought is offered for every day of the month. Begin a day at the appropriate date. Repeat the saying several times: first out loud, then softly, then in a whisper, and then only mentally. With each repetition, allow the words to become absorbed ever more deeply into your subconscious. Thus, gradually, you will acquire a complete understanding of each day's thought. At this point, indeed, the truths set forth here will have become your own.

Keep the book open at the pertinent page throughout the day. Refer to it occasionally during moments of leisure. Relate the saying as often as possible to real situations in your life.

Then at night, before you go to bed, repeat the thought several times more. While falling asleep, carry the words into your subconscious, absorbing their positive influence into your whole being. Let it become thereby an integral part of your normal consciousness.

Day One

The Secret of Love is...

courtesy—which is by no means a mask, but a mark of thoughtfulness and sensitivity. Between two persons who love each other, courtesy, like a delicate waterfall, keeps the mountain pool of their love ever fresh.

Day 2

The Secret of Love is...

respect; for while feelings fluctuate, respect can remain a constant. Listen respectfully to your partner's views when they differ from your own. Preserve a certain dignity in your relationship: that dignity which gives others freedom to be themselves.

DAY THREE

The Secret of Love is...

not making demands of each other.
Love that is not freely given is
bondage.

Day Four

The Secret of Love is...

performing some little act daily to give happiness to your beloved: an act of service, perhaps; a small gift; a word of appreciation; a special smile of affection. Let not the happy brook of your love run dry for lack of replenishing rain.

Day Five

The Secret of Love is...

creativity. Lovingly tend your
relationship, like a garden. Keep it
seeded with fresh interests, fresh ideas,
that it grow always more beautiful.
Weed it, lest the flower beds overrun
with weeds of unconscious habits. For
love to be ever new, it must be
approached creatively, as an art.

Day 6

The Secret
of Love is...

a sense of humor. Share together a sense of the absurd. At the same time, be careful how you tease each other. Never tease if the teasing is unappreciated. Let your humor be kindly, never sarcastic.

Day Seven

The Secret
of Love is...

never losing sight of the underlying
reality of your love. Reflect: Isn't your
long-term relationship more important
than any passing disagreement? Flow
with the longer rhythms of your love.

♥♥

Day Eight

The Secret
of Love is...

not voicing negative emotions, but
waiting for calmness to return to its
post. One who is upset perceives few
things with clarity, though Emotion
parade itself in the garb of revelation.
Calm the heart: Only by so doing can
you perceive things as they really are.

Day Nine

The Secret of Love is...

showing the appreciation you feel. Never take your beloved's awareness of this appreciation for granted. No matter how often you say with sincere feeling, "I love you," though the sentiment is as old as the human race, your words will sound forever fresh and new.

Day Ten

The Secret
of Love is...

holding hands together silently.
Gradually, you will learn to
communicate together telepathically.

Day Eleven

The Secret of Love is...

reverence—less for each other than for Love itself, the eternal gift of God.

Day

12

The Secret of Love is...

paying more attention to the tones of your voice. To magnetize the voice, lift it up from the heart, then release it to soar out through the forehead. Keep the vocal cords relaxed. Your voice will be a delight to listen to if you express through it the calm feelings of your heart.

Day Thirteen

The Secret
of Love is...

speaking more with the eyes — "the
windows of the soul." If you use your
eyes when you speak, it will be as if
those windows were framed with
colorful curtains, making the home
warm and inviting.

Day Fourteen

The Secret of Love is...

holding realistic expectations of one another. For imperfection is inherent in humanity. Concentrate on qualities that have drawn you both together, not on others that might keep you apart.

DAY FIFTEEN

The Secret
of Love is...

non-possessiveness. For one can never truly own another human being. Don't bind your beloved too closely with the cord of your own needs. A plant flourishes when it has free access to air and sunlight.

Day

16

The Secret
of Love is...

not trying to re-shape your partner
into a mold of your own making.
Criticism is corrosive. Accept what *is,*
and you will both be happier. A good
rule is this: Encourage the strengths
you see, but don't either feed or
cauterize the weaknesses.

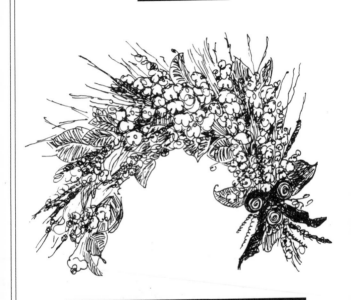

DAY SEVENTEEN

The Secret of Love is...

when misunderstandings occur, not to dwell on how your partner has disappointed you. Ask yourself, rather, what you can do to improve *yourself*, that misunderstandings not arise in future.

Day Eighteen

The Secret of Love is...

for neither of you to assume the role of teacher to the other where personal issues are concerned. On the other hand, be grateful for anything you can learn from each other.

Day Nineteen

The Secret
of Love is...

when you feel inspired to make suggestions, concentrate not on your own need to make them, but on the other's need to hear. Wait even then — months, if need be — until you perceive in your partner a *readiness* to hear what you have to say.

Day Twenty

The Secret of Love is...

sharing with each other your deeper
beliefs, your ideals, your aspirations.

Day Twenty-One

The Secret
of Love is...

stillness. For it is in stillness that love attains perfection. Love is not passion. Human love is a reflection of divine love, and God is perfect stillness.

Day

22

The Secret of Love is...

loving God in each other. Thus you will always feel drawn to the divine perfection behind the human error. For humanity struggles, in the face of countless obstacles and by many and various routes, toward ideals that are eternal.

Day
Twenty-Three

The Secret
of Love is...

expanding your love for each other until it transcends human love, and embraces all humanity, all living beings, all things, as the Creator's handiwork.

Day Twenty-Four

The Secret
of Love is...

giving pleasure to each other, and
not demanding it. For true love is
not desire. The stronger the
passion, the greater its demands;
and the stronger passion's demands,
the greater its emphasis on self-love.
Not in passion, but in tenderness
and kindness love finds its ideal
expression.

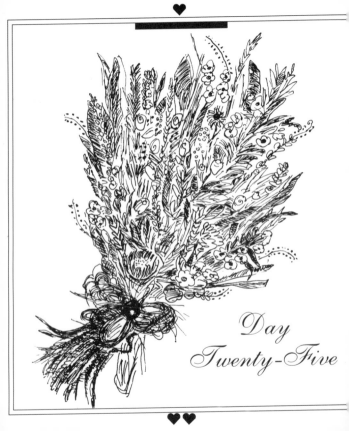

Day
Twenty-Five

The Secret of Love is...

consideration. To whatever extent you are considerate toward others, be even more so to your beloved.

Day Twenty-Six

The Secret
of Love is...

sharing magnetism. The magnetism between you is that subtle power each feels from the other. Only in mutual sharing can this magnetism grow.

Day Twenty-Seven

The Secret
of Love is...

seeking variety in your life together,
and never letting routine chords dull
the melody of your romance.

Day
Twenty-Eight

The Secret of Love is...

seeking opportunities to relax together, sharing your interests and ideas. Depend less on outer stimuli for entertainment. (The louder the noise, the hollower the drum!) Make it a point to be alone together frequently, simply to be yourselves.

Day
Twenty-Nine

The Secret
of Love is...

adaptability. Keep your love fluid, that
it fill every vessel that life places
before you.

The Secret of Love is...

giving strength and comfort to the one you love; receiving strength and comfort gratefully in return, but not demanding them.

Day Thirty-One

The Secret of Love is...

steadfastness: Keep your love immovable, like a high mountain. Keep it ever fertile, like rich soil, through the changing seasons of your lives. And keep it ever central, like the sun as the planets move around it through the vastness of time and space.

Other Books in the **Secrets** Series
by J. Donald Walters

Secrets of Happiness $5.95
Secrets of Friendship $5.95
Secrets of Inner Peace $5.95
Secrets of Success $5.95

Available Spring, 1993:
Secrets for Women $5.95

Available Fall, 1993:
Secrets of Prosperity $5.95
Secrets of Leadership $5.95
Secrets of Self-Acceptance $5.95
Secrets of Emotional Healing $5.95
Secrets of Winning People to Your Ideas $5.95
Secrets of Radiant Health and Well-Being $5.95

Order Form

Use this order form and receive a 20% discount on this purchase. Please fill out the opposite side of this form to complete your order.

QUANTITY	ITEM	PRICE
_____	_____	_____
_____	_____	_____
_____	_____	_____
_____	_____	_____
_____	_____	_____

Subtotal _____

Shipping and Handling

    Up to $10.00 = $3.00
$10.01 to $20.00 = $4.00
$20.01 to $45.00 = $5.00
$45.01 to $55.00 = $6.00
$55.01 to $65.00 = $7.00
$65.01 to $80.00 = $8.00
Over $80.00 = 10% of total

20% discount _____

7.25% sales tax in
California _____

Shipping and Handling
(See chart) _____

☐ Please send me a catalog of
    your books and tapes.

TOTAL _____

Order Form

Please send check or money order and this form to Crystal Clarity, Publishers, 14618 Tyler Foote Road, Nevada City, CA 95959, or call toll free 1 (800) 424-1055.

Name ————————————————————————

Address————————————————————————

City————————————————————————

State———————————————— Zip ——————————

Telephone————————————————————————

Please charge to my credit card: ☐ Visa ☐ MasterCharge

Credit card #————————————————————————

Exp. date————————————————————————